SIMPLE
HOME DÉCOR

14 Easy Craft Projects using Minimalist Design & Maximum Style

LEISURE ARTS, INC. • Maumelle, Arkansas

SIMPLE
HOME DÉCOR

14 Easy Craft Projects using Minimalist Design & Maximum Style

By Lori Wenger

CONTENTS

MEET LORI WENGER

"I've always been a designer of some form or fashion," says Lori Wenger. Lori was a Leisure Arts staff designer for more than seven years, contributing to books in The Spirit of Christmas and Gooseberry Patch series, among others. Since 2012, she has been a contributing photo stylist for numerous Leisure Arts publications.

"My freelance career allows me to work in many different creative genres, from the photo styling, to illustrating, to designing. And luckily I have the continued support of a loving husband and two beautiful children."

Lori's most recent designs published by Leisure Arts include subtle statement jewelry pieces in *Tasseled Jewelry* (#7079), vintage-inspired decorative accessories in *Cool String Art* (#7164) and *Aromatherapy Jewelry* (#7353), a book full of essential oil carrier jewelry. More of Lori's creations may be found on Instagram: lori_wenger.

A NOTE FROM LORI

When Leisure Arts first asked me to create a craft book with simple, minimalist-style projects I was excited to take on the challenge. In all honesty, my style usually isn't minimalist. I tend to gravitate toward layers, texture and pattern. But the idea of simple crafting really appealed to me; why…well, because it's faster! Seriously, there is something incredibly satisfying about starting and finishing a project in a couple of hours! And not only is "simple" fast, it is very on trend right now. Whether you are making to decorate your home, making to give a gift or making just for the sake of making, I hope the projects in this book will inspire you to make something fast, easy and simply beautiful.

M. Lori Wenger

Q & A WITH LORI

What is your favorite ice cream?
Mint Chocolate Chip

What is your favorite music?
I have a pretty eclectic taste in music. I can go from classic rock to 90's alternative to modern folk music depending on my mood.

Do you have any pets?
One 15 year old Chihuahua.

What is your guilty pleasure?
Netflix

What would you do if you had a million dollars?
Make art and not worry about how to sell it.

Do you have an Instagram creative crush?
fancytreehouse…Coury Combs posts just make me happy and she has the most scrumptious color palette.

What's your favorite color?
It changes daily. Today I pick… rosy pink.

What advice would you give a young maker?
Experiment and don't be afraid to make mistakes. Sometimes the best art started out as "mistake."

How do you handle being a "Creative Mama"?
One of my favorite parts of being a mom is creating things with my children. Whether I'm coloring in a color book with my 3 year old or helping my 10 year old film a movie…

What advice would you give your children as they grow up?
Always choose joy! …hmm, I might need to have some t-shirts made with that!

How was your teenage bedroom decorated?
When I was about 14 my mom and I redecorated my room together! I have great memories of planning it all out with her. We choose taupe for the walls (I thought I needed a much more mature color choice than the light baby pink we were painting over). We took down the New Kids on the Block posters and hung framed prints. We moved in an antique armoire, and a white wrought iron bed frame. The bedding was a navy, hunter green and burgundy floral pattern. It was from JC Penny and I loved it. My best friend Beth had the same bedding!

Have any "What was I thinking?" decorating stories?
Tons! I painted my kitchen bright coral…it didn't work at all! Decorating is a creative outlet for me. Sometimes I nail it and a lot of times I fail!

What is your favorite date night?
My favorite date is a simple dinner out, just the two of us. It doesn't have to be fancy. We usually have lots to catch up on. Sometimes I'll make a list on my phone of all the stories from the week that I want to tell him face to face without interruption.

PAINT & GOLD LEAF CANVAS

SHOPPING LIST

- 22" x 28" primed artist canvas

- blue acrylic paint

- gold leaf metal sheets

- white craft glue

- water-based sealer or varnish

- paintbrushes (1", ½" & big fluffy to burnish gold leaf metal sheets)

- painter's tape

- craft knife

- ruler

- pencil

STYLE TIP

The crisp angular lines of this canvas create an energetic vibe for a room.

TO MAKE THE CANVAS

1. Gather your supplies.

2. Lightly sketch out your design of overlapping and intersecting triangles and lineson the canvas. These lines will be covered with gold leaf sheets. Apply tape over the lines, using a ruler to keep the tape straight. Use the craft knife to trim the tape at the corners and points for crisp lines and angles.

3. Paint the canvas; allow to dry and add a second coat of paint if desired.

4. Carefully remove the tape. Apply a smooth, thin layer of craft glue over the pencil lines; allow to dry until tacky. Carefully apply the gold leaf metal sheets, brushing away the excess with a soft, fluffy brush. Lightly buff the gold areas with the fluffy brush. Once the glue is dry, apply a coat of sealer to the canvas.

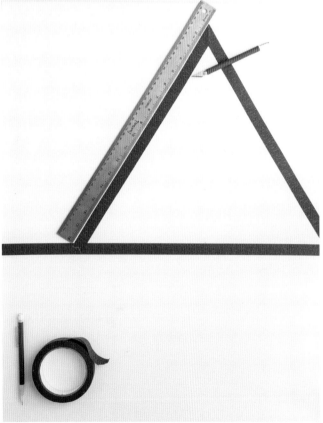

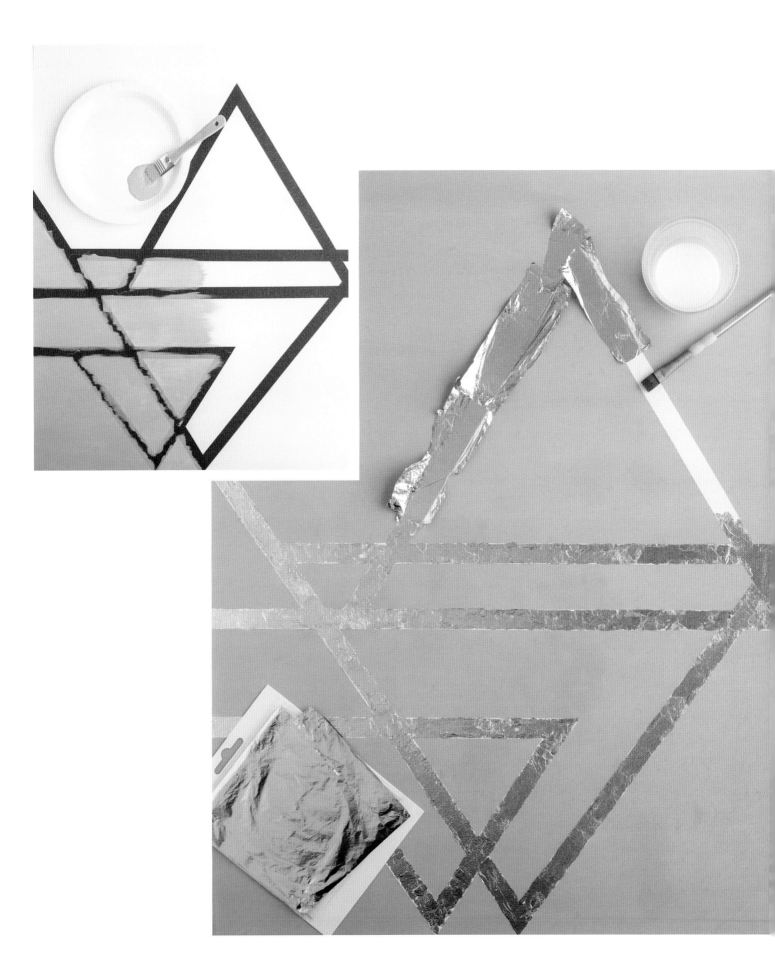

YARN & HOOP WALL HANGING

Finished size: approx. 8"w x 26" l

SHOPPING LIST

- Embroidery hoops (one 6" & one 8")

- yarn (cream & pink/cream varigated)

- 3 ¾" diameter unfinished wood beads

- craft glue

- ruler

- scissors

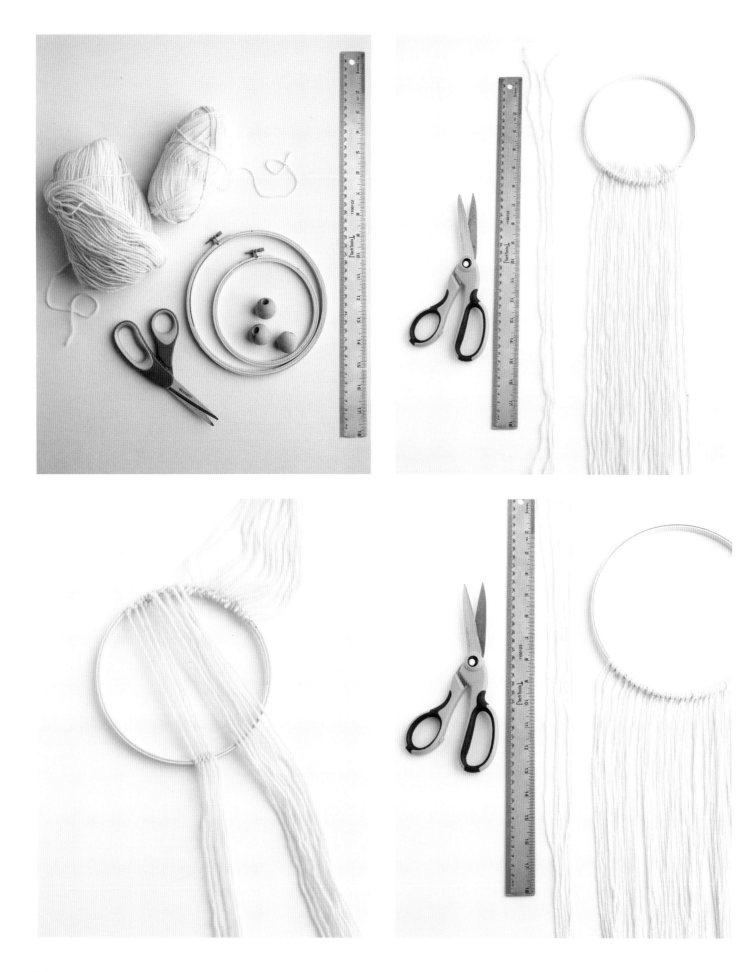

TO MAKE THE WALL HANGING

1. Gather your supplies. You'll only need the inner hoop of each embroidery hoop.

2. Cut 26 pink/cream yarn strands 22" long each. Tie each strand to the small inner hoop. Apply a drop of glue to each knot. When dry, trim the short ends close to the knots.

3. Divide the strands into 2 groups of 13, separating them slightly at the center. Tie each group, strand by strand, to the opposite side of the hoop.

4. Cut 40 cream yarn strands 36" long each. Use a lark's head knot to attach each strand to the large inner hoop.

5. Center the small hoop in the large hoop. Use a lark's head knot and a 24" cream yarn strand to join the hoops at the top center. Thread the beads on the yarn and tie a knot about 4" above the last bead. Trim the yarn ends.

6. Trim the yarn strands to the desired length, trimming the pink/cream strands to a point.

COASTERS

SHOPPING LIST

- 4 balsa wood circles (3½" diameter each)

- acrylic paint (white, pink & chartreuse)

- water-based sealer or varnish

- 1" paintbrush

- rubber bands in various widths

- craft knife

TO MAKE EACH COASTER

1. Gather your supplies.

2. Paint the coaster the desired base color. When first coat of paint is dry, apply a second coat.

3. Place rubber bands on coaster as desired.

4. Paint the coaster a contrasting color, painting over the rubber bands.

5. Once the paint is dry, lightly score the paint with the craft knife along the rubber band edges so that the paint does not come off the coaster when you remove the bands. Remove the rubber bands.

6. Apply two coats of sealer to the coaster.

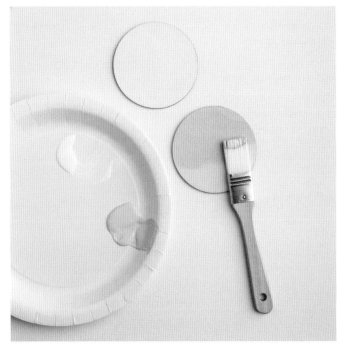

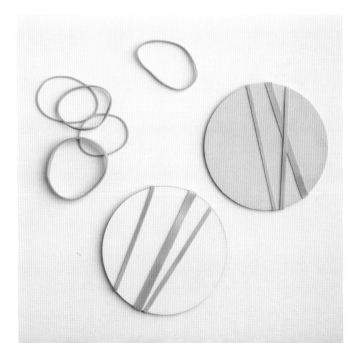

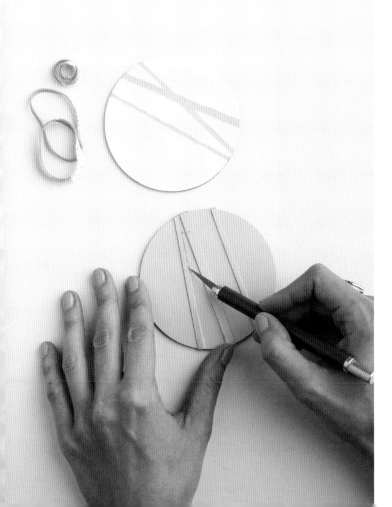

HANGING TABLE

Finished size: 16" long x 10" diameter

SHOPPING LIST

- 10" x ¾" unfinished wood disc with center drilled hole

- 8-12 ¾" diameter unfinished wood beads

- 11 yards cotton cord

- pencil

- ruler

- hot glue gun and glue sticks

- scissors

STYLE TIP

Hemp, twine or nylon cord can be
used in place of the cotton cord.

TO MAKE THE TABLE

1. Gather your supplies.

2. Use the ruler and pencil to draw a plus sign (+) on the wrong side of the wood disc. Cut 6 cord lengths each 64" long. If you want your table to hang longer, cut longer lengths.

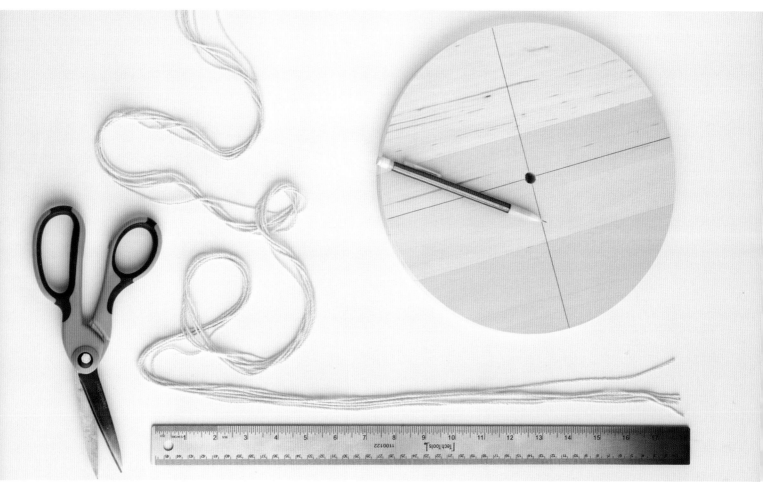

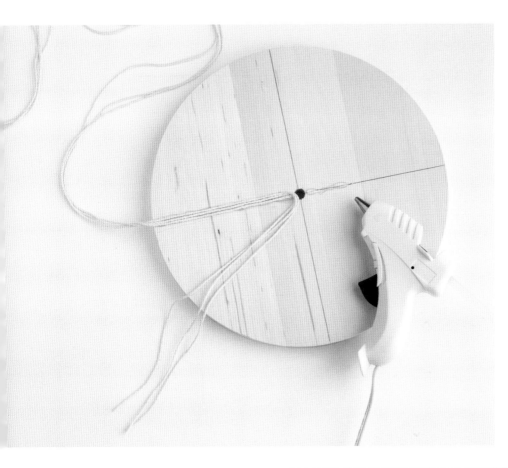

3. Holding 3 lengths together, hot glue the cord to a line on the wood disc bottom, leaving 12" free at the center. Leaving 12" free at the other end, hot glue the cords to the opposite line on the wood disc. Repeat with the remaining cords on the remaining drawn lines.

4. For a hanging loop, tie a knot about 1" below the intersection of all 6 cords at the top. Add beads to the cord ends as desired, tying a knot to hold the bead in place. Trim the cord ends as desired.

MIRRORS

SHOPPING LIST

- 2 wood round plates (12" diameter each)

- 2 round craft mirrors that fit plate centers

- acrylic paint (white & charcoal grey)

- paintbrushes (2", 1" & big fluffy to burnish gold leaf metal sheets)

- gold leaf metal sheets

- white craft glue

- water-based sealer or varnish

- 4 adhesive-backed picture hanging strips

- 1⅜"w painter's tape

- hot glue gun and glue sticks

- ruler

STYLE TIP
Navy and gold would also be a
beautiful color combination!

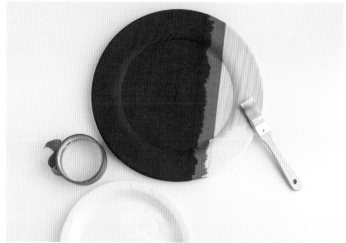

TO MAKE EACH MIRROR

1. Gather your supplies.

2. Place a tape length about 4½" from the plate's edge. Paint the larger side of the plate charcoal grey and the smaller side white. Only applying one coat of paint allows the natural wood grain to show through. After the paint is dry, remove the tape.

3. Place a tape length on either side of the unpainted area. Apply a smooth, thin layer of craft glue to the exposed wood; allow to dry until tacky. Carefully apply the gold leaf metal sheets, brushing away the excess with a soft, fluffy brush. Lightly buff the gold areas with the fluffy brush. Remove the tape.

4. Apply two coats of sealer to the plate.

5. Hot glue the mirror to the plate center.

6. Follow the manufacturer's instructions to apply the picture hanging strips to the wrong side of the plate and on the wall.

MOUNTAINS CANVAS

Finished size: 14" x 18"

SHOPPING LIST

- 14" x 18" primed artist canvas

- acrylic paint (pink, white & charcoal grey)

- ⅜"w metallic gold washi tape

- 3½" diameter circle template (could be wood, cardstock, etc.)

- 1" paintbrush

- painter's tape

- ruler

- craft knife

- pencil

- eraser

TO MAKE THE CANVAS

1. Gather your supplies.

2. Place the circle template on the canvas in the upper right corner. Use the pencil to lightly draw around the circle. Use the pencil and ruler to lightly draw triangle "mountains" along the bottom of the canvas. Some should overlap, one should be tall (12"), one should be short (6"), and the others should fall somewhere in between.

3. Adhere strips of metallic gold washi tape to the canvas for the sun and for the tallest tree. Use the paper you removed from the back of the washi tape to evenly space the gold stripes of washi tape.

4. Being careful to not cut the canvas, use the craft knife and ruler to trim the washi tape that extends beyond the drawn tree lines; trim along the sun lines as well.

5. Tape off the trees that you wish to paint pink. Use the craft knife to trim the tape to smooth points. Paint the trees pink. Mix white paint with the pink paint for a lighter pink color. Once the paint has dried, remove the tape. Tape off and paint the grey tree in the same manner. Erase any pencil marks.

STYLE TIP

If the washi tape doesn't stick well to the canvas, add a bit of craft glue under the tape strip.

31

PAINT CHIP PRINT

Print finished size: 12" x 12"

SHOPPING LIST

- 12" x 12" sheet of white cardstock

- paint chips or cardstock in desired colors (I used 6 colors)

- 1¼" square hole punch

- double-sided tape

- scissors

- ruler

- pencil

- eraser

STYLE TIP

This print is so versatile, it can be framed numerous ways. Here I framed it in a large 22¾" square frame with a 3⅞" mat. On the cover, I chose a frame that just fit the print.

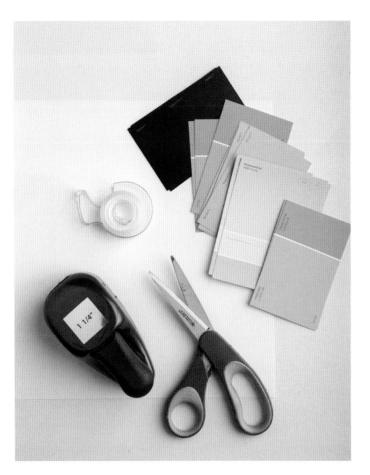

TO MAKE THE PRINT

1. Gather your supplies. Be sure to get enough paint chips/cardstock to punch about 10 squares of each color.

2. Punch about 10 squares of each color.

3. Cut each square in half diagonally to form 2 triangles.

4. Lightly draw a border on the white cardstock sheet about ½" in from all sides. Use double-sided tape to adhere the triangles to the white cardstock, creating desired pattern. Use the ruler to check each row's placement; try not to place a triangle over the outer drawn border. When design is complete, erase pencil lines. Insert the completed print into the frame.

STYLE TIP

There are lots of interesting wood texture cardstock sheets available. How about using different colors and textures of wood for the triangles?

PILLOW

—— Finished size: approx. 18" square ——

SHOPPING LIST

- 18" x 18" white canvas pillow cover with zipper closure

- 18" x 18" pillow insert

- pink acrylic paint

- water-based sealer or varnish

- gold leaf metal sheets

- white craft glue

- paintbrushes (1" & big fluffy to burnish gold leaf metal sheets)

- painter's tape

- 8" square of cardstock for template

- pencil

- ruler

STYLE TIP

If pink doesn't fit into your color scheme, how about a soft green or tranquil blue? I like to pair gold leaf with warm-toned colors and silver leaf with cool-toned colors.

  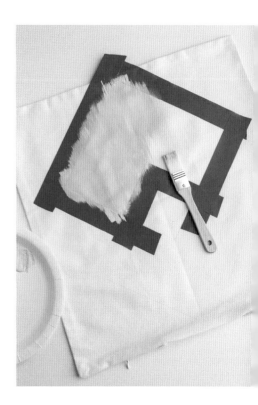

TO MAKE THE PILLOW

1. Gather your supplies.

2. Find the horizontal center of the pillow cover by folding it in half; lightly crease the fold. Turn the cardstock template diagonally and align the points along the pillow cover crease line (be sure the zipper is at the bottom). Draw around the template twice, once aligning the point at the pillow cover bottom and once aligning the point at the pillow cover top.

3. Leaving the small square created by the intersecting larger squares open, tape off the square to be painted. Be sure to press the edges of the tape firmly onto the pillow cover. Paint the square. Remove the tape.

4. Once paint is dry, tape off the other large square. Apply a smooth, thin layer of craft glue within the taped off square; allow to dry until tacky. Carefully apply the gold leaf metal sheets, brushing away the excess with a soft, fluffy brush. Lightly buff the gold areas with the fluffy brush. Remove the tape.

5. Use a ruler to "paint" horizontal lines of glue across the small center square. Apply the gold leaf as you did in Step 4.

6. Brush a thin layer of sealer on the paint and gold leaf. Allow to dry completely. Place the pillow insert inside the pillow cover.

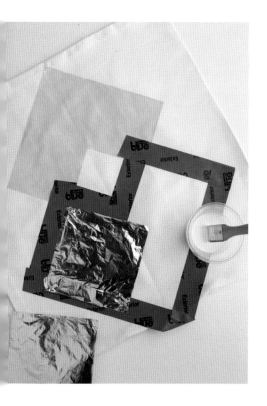
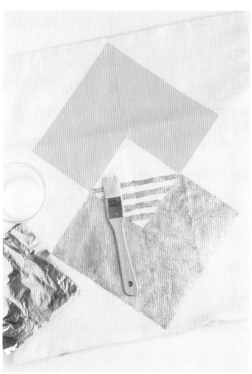

HANGING PLANTERS

Finished planter size: 3⅞"w x 3⅞"d x 3¾"h

SHOPPING LIST

- 2 papier-mache boxes (3⅞"w x 3⅞"d x 3¾"h each)

- white acrylic paint

- water-based sealer or varnish

- 1" paintbrush

- 7 yards jute cord

- 4 1" diameter unfinished ball knobs

- ¾" diameter dot stickers

- painter's tape

- hot glue gun & glue sticks

- ruler

STYLE TIP

Air plants are the perfect low-maintenance plants for these planters.

TO MAKE THE PLANTERS

1. Gather your supplies. You'll only use the boxes, not the lids.

2. Hot glue the ball knobs to the box sides.

3. Place dot stickers around one box bottom. Mask off areas of the remaining box with the painter's tape.

4. Paint the boxes and the ball knobs. When paint is completely dry, remove the tape and dot stickers.

5. Apply sealer to the boxes and knobs.

6. For each box hanger, cut 2 60" jute lengths. Fold a jute length in half and slip over a knob; knot the jute right above the knob. Repeat for remaining knob. Tie the jute ends together about 18" above the box.

PAINT STICK TABLE RUNNER

Finished size: approx. 11⅞"w x 41"l

SHOPPING LIST

- 37 paint sticks (one side must be blank)

- 5½" x 41" piece of natural-colored burlap

- white acrylic paint

- 1" paintbrush

- water-based sealer or varnish

- painter's tape

- cardstock scrap

- tracing paper

- pencil

- craft knife

- scissors

- hot glue gun and glue sticks

TO MAKE THE TABLE RUNNER

1. Gather your supplies. Be sure that one side of each paint stick is blank. Try to find a burlap fabric that is close to the color of the paint sticks.

2. Lay the burlap on your work surface. Center and glue the paint sticks on the burlap, alternating the paint stick ends. Trim away any excess burlap.

3. Draw a diagonal square across the center 3 paint sticks. The side points of the square should be at the edge of the 2 outer sticks. The square will be about 3¼" across the center. Draw a triangle on either side of the square. Trace the pattern (page 64) onto tracing paper and cut out. Use the pattern to cut a cardstock template. Place the template on the runner, aligning the template corner with the corner above. Draw along the diagonal edge of the template. Repeat down the runner and on the remaining sides.

4. Add painter's tape along all the drawn lines. Trim any excess tape with the craft knife.

5. Brush a thin layer of sealer on the inner taped edges. This clear sealer prevents any white paint from bleeding under the painter's tape.

6. Apply the white paint to the runner. Allow to dry overnight. Remove the painter's tape. Apply a coat of sealer to the entire runner.

TRAY

SHOPPING LIST

- 8"w x 12"l x 1⅝"d unfinished wood tray

- 2 1½" diameter unfinished wood ball knobs

- acrylic paint (white, charcoal grey, blue & chartreuse)

- water-based sealer or varnish

- 1" paintbrush

- painter's tape

- ruler

- craft knife

- hot glue gun and glue sticks

STYLE TIP

Apply several coats of sealer
to the tray if you will be
using it to serve drinks.

TO MAKE THE TRAY

1. Gather your supplies.

2. Hot glue the knobs to the tray.

3. Paint the tray and knobs white.

4. Tape off 2 triangles on one end of the tray, making the triangles about 5⅝" tall and 3½" wide. Use the craft knife to trim the tape to smooth points. Paint the triangles charcoal grey. Once the paint has dried, remove the tape. Repeat to paint chartreuse triangles on the opposite end of the tray.

5. Tape off the center diamond. Use the craft knife to trim the tape to smooth points. Paint the diamond blue. Once the paint has dried, remove the tape.

6. Apply sealer to the tray and knobs.

VASES

Finished size: 9" tall x 3¼" diameter

SHOPPING LIST

- 3 9" tall x 3¼" diameter glass vases

- spray paint (white & metallic gold)

- masking tape

- scrap paper

- ruler

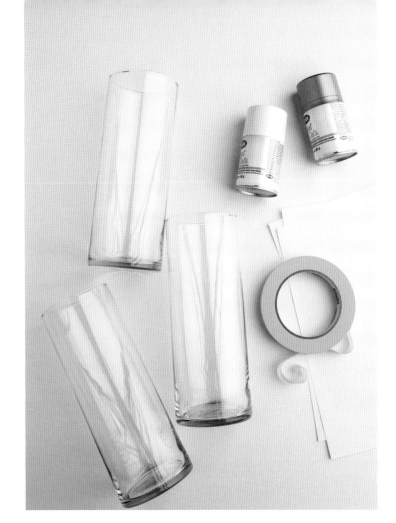

TO MAKE EACH VASE

1. Gather your supplies.

2. Wrap scrap paper around the vase either 4¾" or 2⅜" from the bottom; tape in place. Spray the lower part of the vase white. Let the paint dry at least 24 hours. Don't remove the scrap paper just yet.

3. Place tape strips on the white painted area. This will create the white stripes.

4. Spray the lower part of the vase gold. Let the paint dry for at least 24 hours before removing the tape and paper.

PAINTED WOOD PALLET

Finished size: 15¾"w x 20"l x 1½"d

SHOPPING LIST

- 15¾" x 20" x 1½" pallet-style wood panel

- acrylic paint (blue & black)

- water-based sealer or varnish

- paintbrushes (1" & 2")

- painter's tape

- craft knife

- ruler

- pencil

STYLE TIP

Start by using one coat of paint; this allows the
texture of the wood to show through. If you don't
want to see the wood grain, add an additional coat
of paint after the first one has dried.

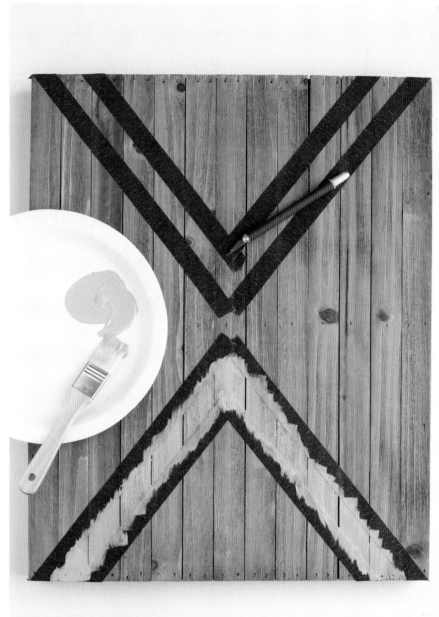

TO MAKE THE PALLET

1. Gather your supplies. Any rectangular-shaped wood piece will work.

2. Use painter's tape to tape off a ¾" wide "triangle" on each short end of the wood panel, aligning the tape at the corners. Use the craft knife to trim the tape at the corners and points for crisp lines and angles. Paint the "triangle" blue. Remove the tape when the paint is dry.

3. Tape off the areas for the black triangles on all four sides and paint. Carefully remove the tape when the paint is dry.

4. Apply sealer to the panel.

SHOPPING LIST

- Assorted wood shapes
  (1⅝" square, 3" circle,
  2" x 3" rectangle, 2 - 2" x 4½"
  rounded rectangles,
  3 - 1" x 2⅝" rounded
  rectangles, 2 - 1⅝" squares &
  2 - 9⁄16" squares)

- light colored jute cord

- ¾" diameter unfinished
  wood bead

- white acrylic paint

- water-based sealer or varnish

- 1" paintbrush

- painter's tape

- hot glue gun and glue sticks

- ruler

- craft knife

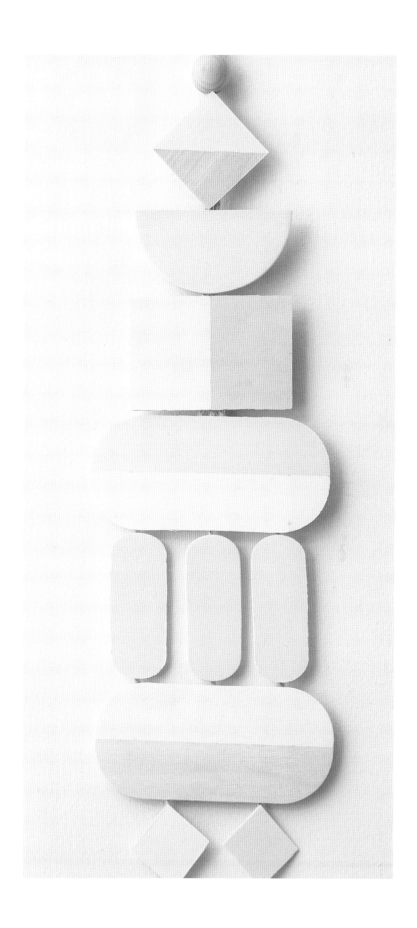

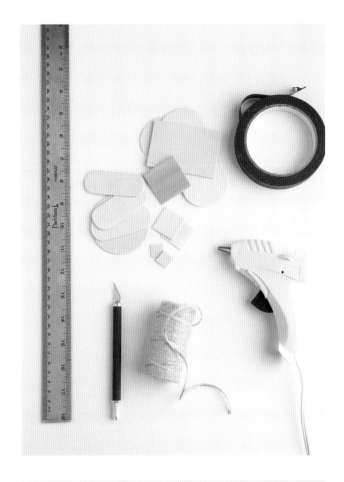

TO MAKE THE WALL HANGING

1. Gather your supplies.

2. Arrange the wood shapes. Use the ruler and craft knife to cut the circle in half.

3. Use tape to mask off areas you would like to leave natural colored. Some pieces are partially painted, some fully painted and some not painted at all. Allow the paint to dry. Remove the tape. Apply sealer to the shapes.

4. Cut an 18" length and a 46" length of jute. Fold the longer length in half; match one end of the shorter length to the fold of the longer end. Tie a knot about 1¾" from the fold. Thread the bead onto all 3 jute strands. Hot glue all 3 strands to the wrong side of the wood shapes, separating the strands to add shapes. Tie an 8" strand to each "tassel". Trim the jute ends as desired.

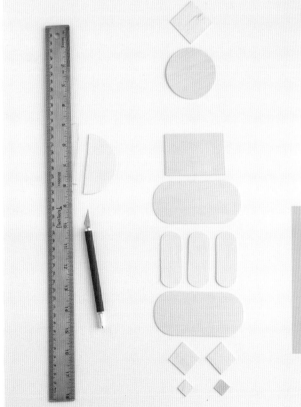

STYLE TIP
Vary the wood shapes to suit your aesthetic. Or, keep adding shapes until the wall hanging is long enough to fit your space.

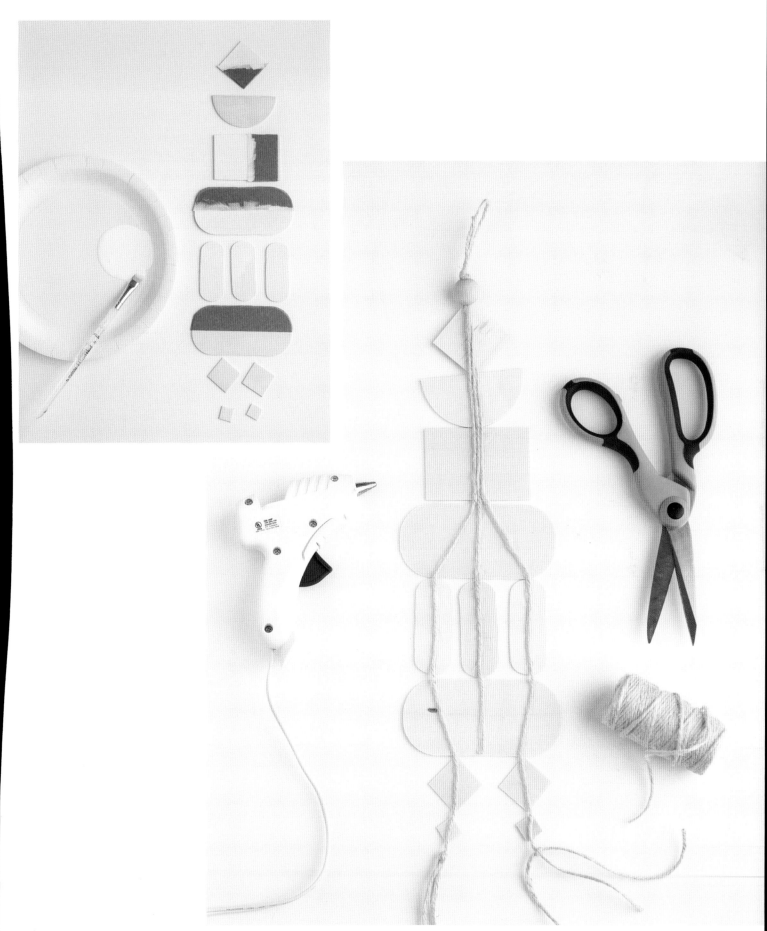

LARK'S HEAD KNOT

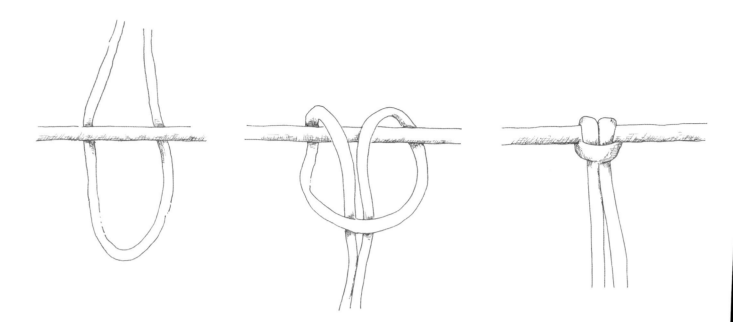

TABLE RUNNER TEMPLATE

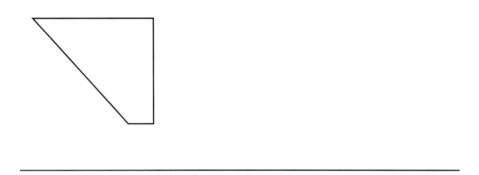

Library of Congress Control Number: 2019933049.

Made in China.

Production Team: Technical Editor – Mary Sullivan Hutcheson; Senior Graphic Artist – Lora Puls; Graphic Designer – Kate Moul; Photo Stylist – Lori Wenger; Photographer – Jason Masters